Contents

1 AMAZING OWLS 1

2 OWL FAMILIES 19

3 PREDATORS AND PREY 35

4 OWL PUKE 49

5 DISCOVER SKELETONS 59

    Rodent Skeleton Reconstruction Chart 71

6 OWL ACTIVITIES (and other cool stuff) 73

    Where to See Owls 78

    Where to Buy Owl Pellets 81

    Owls of North America 82

    Stomachs and Digestion 83

    Bones and Skeletons 86

    Glossary................................. 89

    Acknowledgments 91

remarkable raptors

sky hunters • razor-sharp talon
• **nocturnal** • Great Gray Owl
incredible eyesight • night sig
• **carnivorous** • fringe
feathers • powerful grip • extre
flexibility • **facial dis**
• keen hearing • Long-Eared Owl
reversing toes • strong fe
• molting • Screech Owl • sile
flight • **asymmetrical ears**
lightweight bones • Eurasian Eagle C
• **binocular vision**
ear tufts • many eyeli
• curved beaks • staying co

OWL
PUKE

By Jane Hammerslough

WORKMAN PUBLISHING · NEW YORK

Library of Congress Cataloging-in-Publication Data available upon request

ISBN 0-7611-3186-8

Comic illustrations by Elwood Smith

Technical illustrations by Elayne Sears

Book design and art direction by Janet Parker

PHOTO AND CHART CREDITS: Cover and title page: Mitch Kezar/Getty; Back Cover: Dietrich Gehring; p.1 C.K. Lorenz/Photo Researchers, Inc.; p.2 (left) Gerry Ellis/Minden Pictures, (right) Claus Meyer/Minden Pictures; p.6 Yva Momatiuk and John Eastcott/Minden Pictures; p.8 John Cancalosi/DRK Photo; p.10 R.J. Erwin/Photo Researchers, Inc.; p.11 M.H. Sharp/Photo Researchers, Inc.; p.12 Jeff Lepore/Photo Researchers, Inc.; p.13(top) Dwight R. Kuhn/DRK Photo, (bottom) Gary Meszaros/Photo Researchers, Inc.; p.14 Jacana/Photo Researchers, Inc.; p.16 Wayne Lankinen/DRK Photo, M.H. Sharp/Photo Researchers, Inc., www.naturalexposures.com; p.17 E.R. Degginger/Photo Researchers, Inc., Andy Rouse/DRK Photo, Sid & Shirley Rucker/DRK Photo; p.19 C.K. Lorenz/Photo Researchers, Inc.; p.21 Ron Austing/Photo Researchers, Inc.; p.22 Johnny Johnson/DRK Photo; p.23 Stephen J. Krasemann/DRK Photo; p.24 Michael Durham/DRK Photo; p.25 Michael Quinton/Minden Pictures; Photo; p.27 Tom Evans/Photo Researchers, Inc.; p.28 Joe McDonald/DRK Photo; p.31 Joe McDonald/DRK Photo; p.32 C.K. Lorenz/Photo Researchers, Inc.; p.33 Stephen J. Krasemann/Photo Researchers, Inc.; p.35 C.K. Lorenz/Photo Researchers, Inc.; p.37 www.naturalexposures.com; p.38 Joe McDonald/DRK Photo; p.39 Stephen J. Krasemann/DRK Photo; p.46 (top left) Carolyn A. Mckeone/Photo Researchers, Inc., (top right) Tom McHugh/Photo Researchers, Inc., (bottom) John M. Coffman/Photo Researchers, Inc.; p.47 (top left) Sturgis McKeever/Photo Researchers, Inc., (top right) Kenneth H. Thomas/Photo Researchers, Inc., (bottom) E.R. Degginger/Photo Researchers, Inc.; p.49 C.K. Lorenz/Photo Researchers, Inc.; p.50 Hubertus Kanus/Photo Researchers, Inc.; p.52 Tom & Pat Leeson/DRK Photo; p.53 Dietrich Gehring; p.59 C.K. Lorenz/Photo Researchers, Inc.; pgs.61-64, 65, Dietrich Gehring; Art pgs. 66–67 courtesy of Pellets, Inc.; p.68, 70 Dietrich Gehring; p.73 C.K. Lorenz/Photo Researchers, Inc.; pgs. 74-77, 81 Dietrich Gehring.

Workman Publishing Company, Inc.
708 Broadway
New York, NY 10003-9555
www.workman.com

Printed in the United States of America
First printing: February 2004

10 9 8 7 6 5 4 3 2 1

CHAPTER ONE

AMAZING OWLS

THERE ARE NEARLY two hundred types of owls in the world, ranging in size from the tiny six-inch Elf Owl to the Great Gray and Eurasian Eagle Owl, which both stand over two feet tall. Found on every continent except Antarctica, owls live in a variety of habitats, including tropical rain forest, open prairie, and snowy tundra. The birds nest everywhere from the eaves of suburban malls to trees in remote evergreen forests to underground burrows deep in the desert. Many people think of owls as night birds. It's true that most owls are nocturnal, hunting only at night, but some kinds

OWL INVESTIGATIONS
Quick Quiz

A group of owls is called . . .

A. a *nocturne*

B. a *parliament*

C. a *flock*

D. a *senate*

(Answer is at the bottom of the opposite page)

The Great Horned Owl (left) hunts at night and during the day. The Barn Owl (right) is nocturnal.

of owls hunt at dusk and at dawn, when light is low. There are also a few owl species that are diurnal, hunting during the day. To tell when an owl hunts, look at its eyes. Generally, the lighter the color of an owl's eyes, the lighter it is outside when it hunts. If an owl's eyes are pure black, it means it is strictly a night owl.

Owls have had a reputation for wisdom since ancient times. Perhaps it's because owls sometimes look a bit like human beings. Their intense, direct gaze makes owls look as if they know more than other birds. It's hard to know whether owls are actually more intelligent than other birds, or just appear to be. But one thing is clear—owls have fascinated us throughout human history.

I'm a night owl, baby!

REMARKABLE RAPTORS

O WLS ARE RAPTORS, the group of powerful birds of prey that rule the sky. Raptors (sometimes called "sky hunters") include hawks, eagles, falcons, ospreys, secretary birds, kites, and some vultures. All raptors are carnivores, meat eaters.

As a group, raptors have many special qualities, or adaptations, that enable them to accurately navigate and capture their meals, sometimes from great heights and distances. These adaptations include excellent eyesight and hearing, which help the birds seek out mammals, fish, insects, and other animals—including other birds—to eat.

OWL MYTH

In ancient Rome, the scholar Pliny reported that the ashes of owls' feet were an antidote to snake venom.

(ANSWER: B)

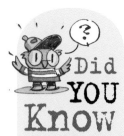

Did YOU Know

A Great Horned Owl could detect the bottom line of an eye chart—from a mile away!

Raptors have powerful feet and toes with razor-sharp talons that they use to grab, kill, and grip prey. Sharp, curved beaks help the birds tear food into strips for themselves or for their young.

Like other raptors, owls are great hunters. But owls are special even among the raptor family. In fact, owls' extraordinary eyes, ears, and feathers set them apart from all other birds in the world.

INCREDIBLE EYES

FROM FLAMINGOS TO PIGEONS, most birds have eyes on the sides of their heads. This eye placement gives birds a wide field of vision and the ability to see in two different directions at once. (Imagine being able to look both ways before crossing a road without turning your head!) But there's a

The small Pygmy Owl has two dark spots on the back of its head that look like eyes.

He never blinks!

MANY EYELIDS

The human eye has two eyelids, upper and lower. But many animals, including crocodiles, horses, polar bears, and dogs, have transparent third eyelids like those of birds to protect the eyes without completely shutting them. Look closely at a dog, and you'll see a whitish membrane in the corner of its eye closest to its nose. If you watch for a while, you may even see the membrane close across the eye. That's the third eyelid at work, moistening the eye.

disadvantage to "wide-angle" eyesight. Most birds have a limited ability to see the same thing with both eyes at the same time. Instead, they look at something with one eye, then the other. (That is why you see birds turning their heads from side to side.) As a result, most birds are limited when it comes to judging depths and distances.

But owls, like humans and other mammals, have eyes on the front of their heads. Their large, forward-facing eyes, give owls better binocular vision than other birds. Binocular vision means that images from each eye overlap, allowing the birds to see in three dimensions. Owls can judge distance, depth, and prey size and speed with precision.

Did YOU Know

Owls' eyes are enormous in proportion to their overall size. A Great Horned Owl's eyes are just about the same size as those of an adult human— but its entire skull is smaller than a baseball.

NIGHT SIGHT

ALL OWLS SEE WELL during the day, but night owls see better in the dark than any animal on Earth. This ability is due to a large number of eye cells, called rods, that are sensitive to low light. Night owls have about five times the number of these cells as humans. Additionally, owls have very large pupils, which are the dark center areas of the eyes. The pupil expands to let in light, and the larger the pupil in any animal's eye, the better it can see at night.

Like other birds, owls have three eyelids: one on top, one on the bottom, and one that moves from side to side across the eye. The third eyelid is a transparent membrane called the nictitating membrane. When the bird flies, its eyes get very dry. But by closing and opening the third eyelid, the

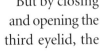

bird can moisten and clean its eyes with tears and still be able to see.

OWL'S-EYE VIEW

A N OWL'S LARGE, POWERFUL EYES are fixed in their sockets like headlights on a car. Unable to turn or roll its eyes, an owl must swivel its entire head to see in different directions. Far exceeding human ability, an owl can rotate its head more than halfway around—about 270 degrees. Some owls are even able to turn their heads completely upside down. How do they do it? You and I have seven neck bones. Owls have fourteen neck bones (the scientific term is cervical vertebrae). This gives the birds extreme flexibility.

To see how far an owl can twist its neck around, imagine turning your neck to look over your shoulder. Now imagine turning until you are looking out over your back. Then, keep going and look over your *other* shoulder. That's about 270 degrees—or three quarters of the way around a full circle.

NIGHT VISION

Owls and other animals such as cats and foxes have much better night vision than humans. If you've ever seen any of these creatures at night, you know that their eyes are reflective. These are eyes that take advantage of every bit of light. Owls may take in one hundred times the light that humans do in dim conditions.

What a head-turner!

A flexible neck does more than allow owls to see from all angles. Owls swivel their heads to *hear* from all angles as well.

SUPERSHARP HEARING

OWLS HAVE THE SHARPEST hearing of all birds on the planet. And no human being would ever win a hearing contest against an owl, either. It may seem strange that owls can hear far better than we do. After all, human ears stick out while an owl's ears are hidden by feathers. But owl ears are designed to catch sounds that humans could never hear.

Try cupping your hand around your ear. Your hand creates a kind of "tunnel" that can help you hear better. In the same way, the stiff

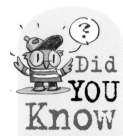

Nope, not ears.

feathers around an owl's face—the facial disk or ruff—form a dish shape that cups sound as well. Just as you might move your cupped hand, the owl moves its facial disk to direct sounds into its ears. A satellite dish works this way to catch airwaves.

Under the feathers, an owl's ears may be completely different from each other in size and position. One ear may be higher or larger than the other. This gives an owl the ability to use its ears one at a time to focus on a sound.

Nighttime in the wild is filled with all kinds of noise. An owl has the ability to tune out chirping crickets and ribbiting frogs and detect the quiet footstep of a mouse. Owls can tell where the sound is coming from by judging the time delay, the split second that it takes a sound to travel from one of its ears to another. If a scuffling vole is to the bird's right, its right ear will

HEAR, HEAR

Dogs, cats, bats, and other animals can hear much higher sounds than people; elephants hear low sounds that humans don't sense. Dolphins and mice have some of the sharpest hearing of any animals, hearing sound frequencies that are five times higher than those humans can hear. While owls use their great hearing to stalk mice, mice use their own excellent ears to sense owls—and make a hasty escape.

TURN IT DOWN!!

I magine being able to hear a person's heart beating, without a stethoscope. Now, imagine hearing the heartbeat, all the time, of every person you meet—along with every other tiny sound they make. It would be enough to drive you crazy. Although an owl can hear the equivalent of a person's heartbeat, its hearing works the way a stethoscope does, registering one sound at a time. Owls' brains respond only to single sounds, so the birds are not overwhelmed by noise.

Ear opening

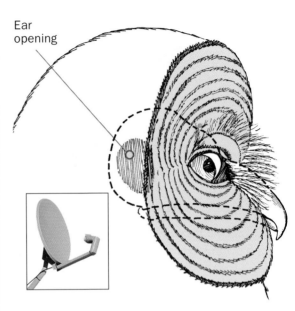

Feathers around the facial disk, or ruff, function like a satellite dish—catching and directing sound.

hear the sound first. A sound coming from above will seem slightly louder in the owl's higher ear; sound waves from below will hit the lower ear first.

To pinpoint the precise source of a sound, the owl uses special skin flaps on either side of its ears. Using muscles, the owl moves these flaps—singly or together—to funnel sound into its ears. By cocking its head from side to side and adjusting its ear flaps, the bird knows exactly where to find the creature making that squeak, scuffle, or chirp.

BIRDS OF A DIFFERENT FEATHER

A N OWL'S WING FEATHERS help make it one of the stealthiest hunters on Earth. The bird's special feathers enable it to fly silently. Even sharp-eared prey often cannot hear an owl coming until it's too late.

Silent wings help an owl hear, too. An owl is not distracted by the sound of its own flapping wings. This allows a flying owl to home in on the faint sounds of faraway prey—even the scuffling of a mouse tunneling under an inch of snow.

How are owl feathers different? Most bird feathers have a crisp, straight line on the edge, which makes a flapping sound when they cut through the air. But owl wing feathers have tiny, soft ridges or serrations, like the teeth of a knife. When you wave one through the air, it doesn't make a sound.

In the world of rapid-moving raptors, owls don't fly especially fast. An owl can fly up to about thirty miles per hour, while some falcons regularly fly at speeds of over one hundred miles per hour. But when it comes to catching prey, the bird more than makes up for its somewhat slow speed with silent flight.

Did **YOU** Know

Owls have about 7,000 feathers.

Serrated feathers make for silent flight.

MOLTING

Like other birds, owls' feathers suffer wear and tear and need to be replaced. Through a process called molting, old feathers drop out and new feathers grow in. Although all of the owl's feathers are eventually replaced, the owl sheds only a few flight feathers at a time, so it is still able to fly and hunt while molting.

FEATHER PROTECTION

How do owls stay dry in the snow or rain? Like all birds, owls have a special oil-producing gland at the base of their tails called a uropygial, or preen, gland. When you see a bird preening, or fixing its feathers with its bill or claws, it's not just spiffing up to look nice for other birds. It is actually spreading oil over its feathers to create a waterproof seal and keep its feathers in smooth flying shape.

Eventually, the oil will wear off. Owls and other birds need to preen regularly to stay weatherproof.

FIGHTING WEIGHT

Raptors and most other birds have light, hollow bones. Still, owl species can be quite large—a Great Gray grows to be more than twenty-four inches tall and has a wingspan of five feet across. So how much do you guess that big bird weighs?

It may be a lot less than you think. Despite their many feathers and substantial appearance, owls are lightweights. Many owl species weigh less than a small box of juice, and most are lighter than a quart of milk. Even the Great Gray—the largest of all North American owl species—only weighs in at about four pounds.

Under the Feathers

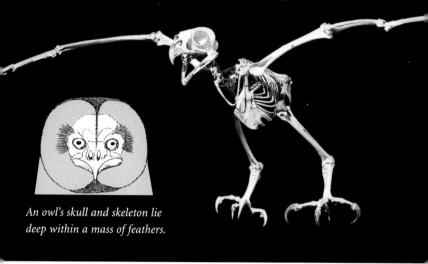

An owl's skull and skeleton lie deep within a mass of feathers.

STAYING WARM AND COOLING OFF

JUST AS BOOTS PROTECT your toes in cold weather, feathers cover the feet and legs of owls that live in cold places to keep them warm. When temperatures are low, owls crouch and fluff their feathers. Young owlets huddle with their mother and brothers and sisters to stay warm.

What about the birds that live in hot places? They have fewer feathers on their legs and feet and stay cool.

When owls are overheated, they open their beaks and pant, just like dogs do.

Is it hot in here?

Amazing! reversible ···· ▸ toes!

The birds also droop their wings down to air out a feather-free area beneath their wings. And on hot days, if there is a stream, lake, pond, or even birdbath nearby, the birds will duck in for a quick dip to cool down.

MY, WHAT BIG TALONS YOU HAVE!

OWLS HAVE FOUR powerful toes with very sharp talons. To handle the incredible impact of snatching, killing, and carrying prey, owls' foot bones are stouter and stronger than those of most other birds. In

FOUR FAMOUS OWLS

HEDWIG, Harry Potter's faithful Snowy Owl. (Snowy Owls don't really live in Great Britain, as Harry's clever friend Hermione points out, but, after all, it's the wizarding world here. Hedwig is Harry's messenger owl

and quite a beautiful, remarkable bird.

Another owl of distinction from another famous magical arena is the legendary . . .

ARCHIMEDES, the owl who accompanies the wizard Merlin in *The Once and Future King* by T. H. White and in the animated Disney movie *The Sword in the Stone.* In the story of the boy who grows up to become King Arthur, first ruler of the British Isles,

fact, they have the greatest gripping strength of all birds of prey.

Like other birds, owls have three toes that face forward, and one that faces backward. But owls have something very special: amazing reversing toes. When the bird is perched or clutching prey, one of its front toes swivels to the back. With two toes in the front and two in the back, the bird uses its talons like a sharp, precise pincer to get a great grip on a tree branch—or on dinner.

An owl's feet are more than just super strong. Their soles are also made for keeping a grip—and for withstanding wear and tear in the wild. Think of the bumpy treads on the bottom of a pair of boots. They help you get through snow, ice, or rocky terrain without falling flat on your face. Now imagine having a similar sort of rough surface on the soles of your feet. That's what owls have all the time, naturally.

BUILT-IN COMB

Barn Owls have a special foot-feature: a comblike middle claw. The bird uses its fine-toothed, serrated talon as a preening comb to spread oil through its feathers.

Merlin tutors the boy with wise Archimedes perched on his shoulder! And of course, who could forget . . .

WOL, or **OWL,** from A. A. Milne's *Winnie the Pooh* books. Fond of large words and the sound of his own voice, he inspires Pooh's admiration. "'If anyone knows anything about anything,' said Bear to himself, 'it's Owl who knows something about something.'"

Speaking of knowledge, which beloved bird sets sail with a fabulous feline? If you guessed . . .

THE OWL of "The Owl and the Pussycat," you're right! Since this poem by Edward Lear was first published in 1871, people have been trying to figure out just what a "runcible spoon" is. Never mind. The famous fictional friends still live on, dancing by the light of the moon.

Whooo hoots
.... or howls?

meow!

Who cooks for youuu?

cackle . . .

SNOWY OWL

BARRED OWL

LONG-EARED OWL

The bird known as the White Terror of the North has a loud, booming call to establish territory, and also hisses, rattles, and cackles to scare away intruders.

Sometimes called a "hoot owl," this bird sounds like it is saying, "Who cooks for you? Who cooks for you all?"

If you ever hear a low, mysterious moan or a high-pitched meow in the woods at night, a Long-Eared Owl may be nearby.

woof?

The Barred Owl hoots and may even call back to you if you "hoo-hoo-hoo-hooooo" at it. But did you know that the calls of other owl species sound like barking, whistling, chirping, hissing, growling, wailing, or even blood-curdling, human-sounding shrieking? Here are some North American owls and their unforgettable voices:

arf!

GRRR!

cooo!

SHORT-EARED OWL	BARN OWL	SCREECH OWL
While the Long-Eared Owl sometimes sounds like a cat, the Short-Eared Owl's call sounds like a howling dog. Its barklike call? "Hee-yow!"	This creature's shrieking voice sounds like human screaming. Barn Owls like to roost in deserted country houses and barns, so their calls have given rise to many stories of ghosts and haunted houses.	Only baby Screech Owls screech. Adults make soft, rhythmic calls that sound like the cooing of a dove or the neighing of a horse.

hooting • home territory
shelter • courting • Snowy Ow
• sky dancing • night duets
roost • nuzzling feathered face
• Burrowing Owl • hom
for a family • gifts of food
round eggs • incubatin
• nestmates • egg tooth • Elf Owl
downy owlets • bite-size snack
• "I'm hungry!" • beak to beak
Great Horned Owl • learning to fl
• protective parents
leaving the nest • a new famil
• a clutch of chicks • fledglings
hunting lessons • flockin
together • sibling rivalr

CHAPTER TWO

OWL FAMILIES

I T BEGINS WITH A SINGLE HOOT in the night and may last a lifetime: When many owls choose a mate, it's for good. Once they are a year or two old, most owls are ready to settle down with a mate. Some owls call back and forth to each other for weeks, then hoot in duet—but only when they've found just the right bird.

Soon after the owls pick a partner and mate, it's time to raise a family. And what a family! Keeping a clutch of hungry little owlets full and happy is quite a challenge. The owls' solution? Both males and females pitch in with parenting.

Did YOU Know

The word *owl* comes from *ule,* an Old English word that means "to howl."

OWL-FASHIONED DATING

WANT TO HEAR AN OWL CALL? Try listening in the fall, when male birds establish their home territories by proclaiming with a few good hoots, "This is my turf—don't mess with it!" Even better, keep your ears open during late winter and early spring evenings, when the young owl's attention turns to young female owls. The owl calls you hear then are signaling the start of mating season.

Some of that hooting may sound like horrible howling to you, but other owls of the same species find it irresistible. The birds begin calling back and forth, and soon they move closer to each other to see what that other attractive-sounding owl actually looks like.

That's when the serious bird-flirting begins and, for many species, that means

CLAIMING TURF

Before they begin looking for a mate, male owls must stake out their own hunting territory. When they find a good spot, the birds hoot to claim the space. If another male answers the call, the owl will either leave to seek out another space, or confront the current resident and try to chase him out. Owls defend their own territories fiercely, so unless the current resident is very weak, the owl must look for another place to claim as his own.

This happy couple is a pair of Saw-Whet Owls.

giving an air show. Both the male Short-Eared and Snowy Owl clap their wings while flying to show off for females, and females respond with calls. Some owls perform a special circling flight in the air to invite a potential mate home.

All this dramatic behavior serves an important purpose. As he swoops through the air, the male is showing the female his hunting territory. The female responds with calls to let him know that she is interested in him and where he lives. If the female joins him in flying, it's a signal that she would like to see more of what the male owl has to offer.

The next step for the male owl in courting a young female is leading her to the

SLEEPY TIME

Owls sleep at various times during the day. Most owls simply droop their heads down on their chests to doze off. But some small species snooze after twisting their heads around and tucking them under their back feathers. Though most owls aren't social, some species, such as the Short-Eared Owl, sleep together in a flock.

Great Horned Owls have taken over this abandoned nest.

roosting site that he has chosen. The choice of roosting site is important because it is where owls spend most of their lives while raising baby owls. A good site offers shelter from the elements and is hidden from possible predators. If the female owl likes what she sees, she will follow the male to his roost.

COURTING

ONCE THE BIRDS are together at the nesting site, they communicate with each other in many different ways, from standing a certain way to touching and making special sounds. Some male owls stamp their

Owl Homes

Although Burrowing Owls dig nests in the ground that they line with grass and plant materials, most owls do not build nests. Instead, they create a makeshift twig pile on the ground or move into hollow trees, rock crevices, barns, or other buildings. Owls also take over nests that eagles, hawks, crows, and other animals have abandoned. Most owls that migrate during the winter return to the same nesting site each year.

Burrowing Owls nesting on the prairie.

feet. That tells the female, "This is a great place to raise a family!" Most owl species then touch and preen each other. During this time, many kinds of owls click their tongues, fence with their beaks, and nuzzle their faces against one another—something like humans dancing cheek-to-cheek.

Finally, it's the big moment: Will she or won't she take that owl to be her mate for life? Among many owl species, the male presents the female with a dead rodent or other treat to show he'll be a terrific provider. Once the female accepts that furry wedding present, it's a done deal. The two birds are a genuine couple.

Did YOU Know

To clean up, owls like to take baths —both dust baths and the regular kind in water.

BIG GIRLS

BIG GIRLS

Female owls are usually bigger than male owls—up to 30 percent bigger. Some scientists believe the female is larger so she can shield and protect young owlets in the nest while the male is off hunting for food for his family.

OWL COUPLES

ONCE A MALE AND FEMALE owl become a couple, most will live in the same place for the rest of their lives. As they raise their young season after season, they remain in the same home territory.

Owl couples care for each other by grooming each other's feathers. Scientists call this "mutual preening." Mutual preening isn't just useful for the birds to stay clean. Scientists also believe it is important in helping adult birds bond as a couple—and that it is fun for the birds, as well.

Honey,
I'm home!

Like other birds, owls use their beaks to comb through their body and wing feathers to remove dirt and spread oil from the uropygial gland (see page 12). To groom the facial disk feathers, owls use their talons.

When Barn Owls preen each other, the female first approaches her mate while making little whistles or squeaks. She then preens him from top to toes, but especially around the face and the back of the head. The male then preens the female. As they preen each other, the owls make little twittering sounds and chirrups. Once they are all cleaned up, both birds doze off.

Downy owlets hatching from eggs.

INCUBATING EGGS

THE FEMALE BEGINS to lay eggs soon after the owls mate. Most owls lay a single round, white egg every few days. A group of owl eggs is called a clutch. The average owl clutch has five eggs, but the number depends on the species and how much prey is available at the time. More food usually means more eggs.

Not all the birds inside the eggs will survive to become juvenile owls. In a Barn Owl's clutch, for instance, about 30 percent may survive to become fledglings.

The female begins incubating her eggs as the baby birds grow inside the shells. Female owls and other birds have a special brood

OWL INVESTIGATIONS

Quick Quiz

Tiny desert-dwelling Elf Owls often nest...

A. in the sand

B. on top of telephone poles

C. in old woodpecker holes in giant saguaro cactuses

D. on top of giant saguaro cactuses

(Answer is at the bottom of this page)

(ANSWER: C)

A young owl spends time under its mother's wing.

OWL INVESTIGATIONS

A group of baby birds in a nest is called . . .

A. a *brood*

B. a *featherlette*

C. a *pillow*

D. an *aviarita*

(Answer is at the bottom of this page)

patch, a featherless area on their bodies where eggs are kept warm.

In some owl species, the male takes turns sitting on the eggs. But most of the time, the male is out catching prey for himself and his mate. In the meantime, back at the nest, the female is busy turning and rearranging the eggs (as often as every twenty minutes) with her beak and face so they warm evenly.

AWESOME OWLETS

AFTER ABOUT FOUR WEEKS, the first baby owl (also called an owlet or owl chick) appears in the nest. Like other baby birds, owlets break out of their shells using a special egg tooth. The egg tooth is a small, hard bump on the top of an owlet's beak that it uses like a built-in chisel to tap through its shell. Soon after the bird hatches, the egg tooth falls off.

At birth, a baby owl is a weak, blind, down-covered, damp little creature that is totally dependent on its parents for shelter, protection, warmth, and food. In fact, new-born owlets are so frail that they sometimes have difficulty even holding up their large heads. For the first two or three weeks of their lives, owlets huddle together under their mother's wings and body to stay warm and hide from possible predators.

While the owl mother stays with the owlets in the nest those first couple of weeks, the male bird becomes a fast-paced food delivery service for his family. Many times a night, he captures prey, brings it home, then goes right back out again for more. Although the tiny owl chicks can eat whole insects, they are not yet ready to swallow the fur or bones of larger prey. The mother owl uses her claws and beak to tear boneless, bite-size pieces for her babies. Then the owlets take the meat from their mother, beak to beak.

Did YOU Know

The larger the owl, the larger the egg. Great Horned Owls have eggs the size of chicken eggs, while those of the little seven-inch Pygmy Owl are half that size.

They're so immature!

FIRST FLIGHTS

An owl cannot fly until its tail and wing feathers have grown in fully. Larger owl species have more feathers and take longer to fledge than smaller species, so their owlets' first attempts at flying occur later. While a tiny Elf Owl can fly within a month of hatching, a Barn Owl is usually two months old before it takes to the air, and a Great Horned Owl is often older than that before it can fly.

Owlets are born days apart.

GROWING UP FAST

BY THE TIME THE OWLETS are about two weeks old, their eyes are open, they are covered with thick down, and some are able to eat whole prey. Though they no longer spend all of their time underneath their mother, the owlets still huddle with her and each other. Not yet able to fly but growing fast, the babies have huge appetites, and begin to produce pellets, just as adults do.

When owls are about a month old, they are able to run and even try flying. Their down begins to fall off, replaced by feathers that grow in gradually, everywhere from their wings to their distinctive facial disks. This process is called fledging. When the baby bird has all its adult feathers, it is a full-fledged owl.

Owl babies grow quickly. By the time a Barn Owl owlet is forty days old, it can weigh as much as its parents, but it still can't hunt for itself. Both parents are kept very busy through the night flying back and forth to the nest with prey for their young.

BIG EATERS

FOR LITTLE ANIMALS, baby owls can really pack it away. A study of Barn Owls found that owlets who weren't much more than a month old ate about four small animals a night. Multiply that by five babies in a nest, and you can see why owls parents work so hard.

OWL INVESTIGATIONS

Quick Quiz

A group of eggs that an owl lays is called . . .

A. a *clutch*

B. a *flush*

C. a *straight*

D. a *sloop*

(Answer is at the bottom of this page)

A Barn Owl may provide its young with more than twenty rodents in a single night!

(ANSWER: A)

Did YOU Know

In the first month or so of life, kittens and puppies may double or triple their weight over several weeks. But a scientist studying Great Gray Owls found the weight of one of the owlets increased from 40 grams to 225 grams in a single week!

In fact, owl parents put so much work into hunting prey for their offspring that their babies soon weigh more than *they* do. Imagine if you weighed more than your mom or dad when you were still just a tot.

Owlets are busy, too. Starting when they are about a month old, Barn Owl chicks, like other owlets, begin to explore the world outside the nest. Before they can fly, baby owls walk, hop from branch to branch, flap their wings, and begin to learn calls. With a careful watch on their babies, parents begin to teach owlets about hunting. When they are about eight weeks old, they begin to fly and are ready to hunt prey for themselves.

LEAVING THE NEST

To become good hunters, owlets must practice again and again. Although the birds may begin to catch prey soon after learning to fly, they still cannot survive on their own. For several weeks or months, owl parents still feed the owlets as their hunting skills improve.

As the owlets get bigger, it begins to get very crowded at home. Although a few owl families stay together over the winter, young birds of most species are ready to leave the nest anytime from midsummer to early fall.

It's then the young owls' turn to strike out on their own, calling out into the night to establish their own territories. When owlets are a year old, they may begin looking for a mate of their own.

Some owls stay close to their parents, in the same home territory. Others establish their own territory as far as a hundred miles away. Meanwhile, back at the old nest, the female has laid another clutch of eggs, and another group of baby birds may be hatching.

OWL SIBLING RIVALRY?

Owlets are very competitive. Baby birds grab food out of one another's mouths, often having a tug-of-war with partially swallowed pieces of meat. Like humans, birds that are born first are stronger than those born later, and often win the battle. (And you thought the sibling rivalry was bad in your family!)

Barn Owl nestmates.

Owl Defense

Although adult owls have few predators, owlets are not able to defend themselves from other animals. (Interestingly, some of the animals that prey on baby owls—including snakes, squirrels, opossums, and other birds—are those that larger owls hunt themselves.) Owl parents are loyal and protective—and have some ingenious ways of keeping themselves and their families safe. Here are some ways the birds protect themselves and their babies:

THE "SLOB"

European Pygmy Owls let pellets, poop, eggshells, and other trash build up at the entrance to their nesting sites. This keeps predators from getting too close to the nest. Similarly, Burrowing Owls collect dog poop and put it in front of their burrows.

THE "ALL-OUT STRIKE"

Both male and female owls will dive and tear at animals that make a move to hurt them or their families. Using their sharp beaks and claws, the birds launch a full-force attack to vigorously defend their homes and offspring.

THE "BLOW-OUT"

If a predator is pursuing an owl, the bird fluffs outs its feathers, spreads its tail and wings, and makes scary hissing or snapping sounds.

THE "VOICE-OVER"

To repel predators from their nests, Burrowing Owls and owlets make a distinctive hissing noise that sounds exactly like a rattlesnake.

THE "FAKE-OUT"

Owls often distract possible predators away from their nests and babies by acting injured or even playing dead. Favorite techniques include limping pathetically, dragging their wings, and lying still and stiff on the ground.

THE "SNOOZE"

Some owls pretend to be asleep when a predator is near. Then the faking owl will launch a surprise attack on the unsuspecting intruder.

"MASTER OF DISGUISE"

When a possible predator is nearby, many kinds of owls stand perfectly still, pull their wings in close to their bodies, narrow their eyes, and move close to a tree trunk to blend in with their surroundings.

night hunters • surprise attacks
mice • pinpointing prey • bug
• perch, search, pounce! • rats
Pygmy Owl • flying in for dinne
• under snow • voles • precis
strike! • shrews • grabbing a meal
reptiles • Barred Owl • dinne
delivery service • skunks • fo
web • habitat • migration • starling
• Flammulated Owl • fier
predators • weasels • moles
swooping • helpful to humans • ey
shut • sticky tongues • missin
the target • day and night hunters
lizards • amazing diet

CHAPTER THREE

PREDATORS AND PREY

MAGINE EATING 80 QUARTER-POUND HAMBURGERS. Now, think about munching that much several times in one evening. Some owls eat their own body weight, or even more, in prey night after night. Owls may search for food on the wing or perch-and-pounce, watching and listening from above, then swooping down to capture prey. All owls are experts at surprise attacks, striking at rodents and other animals when they least expect it.

THE HUNT

FLYING OR PERCHING above the ground, an owl begins its hunt by scanning the area below with its excellent eyesight. The bird then uses its sharp ears to determine the exact location of a particular vole, mouse, insect, or other creature that might be scurrying along.

Once it has found a possible meal, the owl stares directly at its target and begins its attack flight.

As the owl flies or glides toward its target, the owl stretches its wings wide. Eyes never leaving its target, the bird prepares to strike by bringing its strong feet forward.

Some species, such as Barn Owls, swing their long legs back and forth like a rhythmic pendulum as they home in on their prey. Others bend their heads far over their feet just before they strike.

With one foot aimed to simultaneously stun and hook the prey's head,

FACE-PLANT!

The Great Gray Owl can hear a possible meal that's more than a foot deep in snow. The bird dives and plunges its long legs deep into the snow to grab prey. But what happens to the rest of the bird as its feet plunge down? Like a fallen snowboarder, the bird does an icy face-plant in the snow's surface.

Eyes on the prize: Great Horned Owl prepares to strike.

and the other poised to strike its hindquarters, the owl goes in for the capture and kill. Spreading its strong toes and talons wide, the bird quickly grabs the creature. The prey is often paralyzed and killed on impact, as the owl strikes down on the creature with its sharp talons. Covering the prey with its wings,

the owl swiftly uses its beak to break the prey's neck.

If hunting only for itself, an owl may immediately swallow the prey right there on the spot. But if it is hunting for its family, the owl will deliver the prey to the nesting site —and soon set out again.

Did YOU Know

Owls eat lizards, frogs, toads, and other amphibians. Eurasian Eagle Owls consume monitor lizards—which can grow to ten feet long and weigh more than 300 pounds. The birds only eat the smaller ones, though.

Eastern Screech Owl eating a minnow.

WEATHER MATTERS

During the winter, seeds and other food from plants may be impossible to find. If rodents and other animals die because they can't find food, then owls will starve as well. As a result, some owl species migrate in the fall to warmer places, where food is more plentiful. Like other birds, owls may fly far away from their home territory—sometimes 1,000 miles away. Once the weather begins to change in the spring, the birds fly back home to nest and mate.

ALL YOU CAN EAT

M OST OWLS EAT rodents, moles, shrews, and the occasional small bird and large insect. But, depending on their size and environment, some owls have an amazingly varied diet:

Flammulated Owl—These small owls live on beetles, moths, caterpillars, spiders, centipedes, and other bugs. An especially fine catch for a Flammulated Owl? A scorpion.

Great Horned Owl—Sometimes preying on owls of other, smaller species, the Great Horned Owl also takes its prey large. Mammals such as skunks, woodchucks, and big birds—including geese and herons—are part of this huge owl's diet.

Pygmy Owl—This fearless, tiny owl attacks creatures much larger than itself—and can carry three times its own weight in prey. Hunting during the day, Pygmy Owls capture birds, lizards, and snakes, along with rodents and insects.

Burrowing Owl—Another small, intrepid hunter, the Burrowing Owl goes after some big prey, including young prairie dogs and rabbits, gophers, and bats.

Snowy Owl—Dwelling in northern regions, these owls snack on snowshoe hares

INSECT-I-SNACKS!

F rom caterpillars to full-grown moths, from beetles to grasshoppers, owls are big insect-eaters. Naturally, nocturnal birds eat nocturnal bugs, and those owls active in the daytime snack on the flying, crawling, and hopping creatures you see during the day.

and lemmings, along with other small mammals.

Barred Owl—Barred Owls are opportunistic feeders—meaning they'll eat anything available. Their broad diet includes frogs, salamanders, fish, moles, even other owls—including those larger than themselves.

PREYING ON RODENTS

THEY'RE THE LARGEST GROUP of mammals in the world and live on every continent except Antarctica. Their teeth never stop growing—and they never stop gnawing on things. They eat crops and many carry lice, ticks, fleas, and other parasites that spread nasty—even deadly—diseases. But without them, owls and many other animals couldn't survive.

A rodent family reunion.

Blind Strike

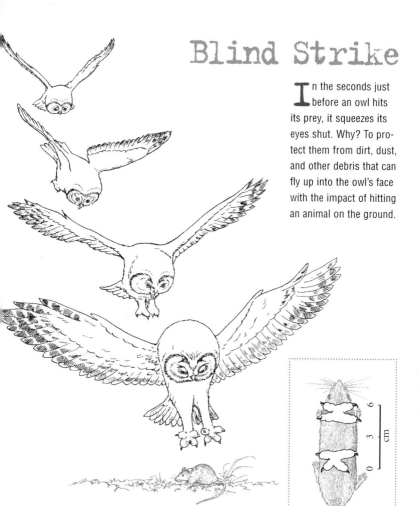

In the seconds just before an owl hits its prey, it squeezes its eyes shut. Why? To protect them from dirt, dust, and other debris that can fly up into the owl's face with the impact of hitting an animal on the ground.

6
3
0
cm

FLY, FLY AGAIN!

Owls often must make several attempts to catch prey. Even though they have superb hunting skills, they sometimes miss their targets.

The owl aims its talons at its prey's hindquarters and neck, which often break on impact.

One shrew species is less than an inch long—believed to be the smallest mammal on Earth.

Meet the rodents. This group of animals includes mice, rats, voles, chipmunks, squirrels, prairie dogs, lemmings, beavers, muskrats, porcupines, chinchillas, and woodchucks, among others. And if you keep a hamster, gerbil, or guinea pig as a pet, you're a rodent owner.

While owls eat all kinds of rodents, they usually prey on members of the *Myomorpha*, or mouselike, group. These include voles, lemmings, mice, and rats—and they constitute one quarter of all mammal species in the world. Myomorphae reproduce at an astonishing rate. In a single year, a rat may bear more than sixty young, which means lots of good eating for owls.

MOLES AND SHREWS

OWLS ALSO PREY ON OTHER kinds of small furry animals. Two of the most commonly found in pellets are the mole and the shrew.

Moles and shrews are not rodents. The mole is a member of the *Talpidae* family, a group that mostly lives in underground tunnels. The shrew is part of the *Soricidae* family and is one of the hungriest animals on earth. A shrew needs to feed night and day to stay alive.

OWL MORTALITY

A DULT OWLS ARE seldom attacked and killed. Few owls die of old age or other natural causes, either.

Humans are an owl's greatest threat. Accidents with cars and wires are a leading cause of death for owls. Pesticides—chemicals used to kill insects or rodents—also kill owls. When owls eat prey that have eaten or been exposed to poisons, the owls are poisoned as well.

Similarly, when an owl's habitat changes or is destroyed through land development, it harms the birds. With no place to live and less food to eat, the owl must quickly find a new home and food source—or die.

Some animals, including some owl species, are specialized eaters. That means their diet consists of one thing. Most owls eat a variety of prey, which helps their chances of survival.

STICKY TONGUES

A n owl's tongue has tiny barbs on it to help hold on to prey as it swallows it whole.

The Barn Owl mostly eats mice, shrews, voles, rats, and moles. Occasionally, the owl might also eat another bird or insect.

Plants produce seeds, which mice, voles, insects, and other animals eat.

Starlings and other birds eat plants, small reptiles, worms, insects, and seeds.

Insects eat plants, other insects, seeds, and animal materials (including owl pellets).

Shrews eat worms and insects.

The owl's prey eats snails, salamanders, and other creatures.

Moles eat insects, worms, and slugs.

Owls produce pellets, which provide shelter and food for insects. Pellets also enrich the soil, feeding plant life.

FOOD CHAINS AND FOOD WEBS:

A LL LIVING THINGS need energy to survive—and all living things are part of one or many food chains and webs.

Food chains make a straight line. Plants get energy from the sun. Seeds grow on plants. Mice eat seeds. Owls eat mice.

A food web is made up of many food chains. A food web shows the connections, some of them surprising, between plants and animals, predators, and prey.

Why are owls at the top of the food chain and web? Owls' vision, hearing, and quiet flight help them avoid other animals' attacks.

moles

snails and slugs

worms

plants and seeds

owl pellets

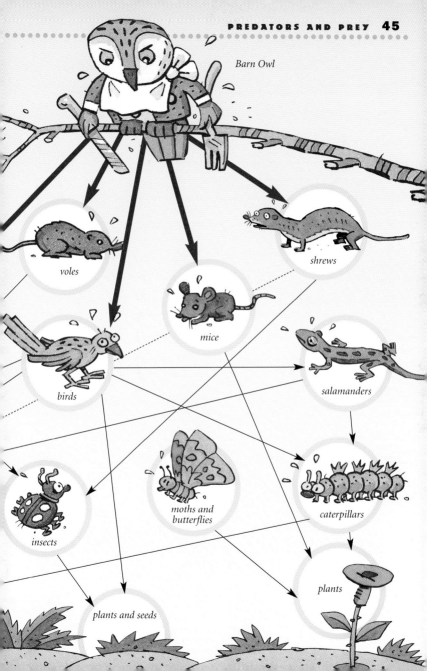

Barn Owl

voles

shrews

mice

birds

salamanders

moths and
butterflies

caterpillars

insects

plants

plants and seeds

Common  Prey

mouse

rat

MOUSE	VOLE	RAT

Mice are brown or gray, with large ears, pointed muzzles, and small eyes. These nocturnal rodents are between five and seven inches long, including a tail that is three to four inches long. Found in fields, forests, barns, and other buildings, mice are omnivores, eating any available food, including seeds, grains, vegetables, and meats. A single mouse can eat eight pounds of food in a year. A mouse can travel at a speed of twelve feet per second.

Sometimes called "field mice," voles have round muzzles and small ears. They have stockier builds and shorter tails than mice. Species include grayish-brown meadow voles and water voles. Voles range from three to seven inches long and live in pastures, meadows, grassy areas, and near bodies of water. They clear runways leading to their underground burrows for quick escape from predators.

With black, brown, or reddish fur, nearly all rats have long, hairless tails, and bodies that are seven to ten inches long. While the noses and muzzles of black rats are pointed, those of brown rats are blunt. Rats survive in a wide variety of climates and environments, from cities to mountains to open plains. These rodents can swim a mile, withstand falls of 20 feet, and are able to gnaw through cinder block, wood, and even metal in search of food.

vole

Profiles

shrew

starling

SHREW	MOLE	STARLING

Although they resemble soft, gray-brown mice, shrews are distinguished by their long, pointed faces. Many species also have red-tipped teeth. North American short-tailed shrews are between three and four inches long, with short, inch-long tails. Living everywhere from deserts to grasslands to forests, shrews eat plants, insects, worms, and amphibians. Fierce hunters, shrews kill prey many times their own size.

Moles burrow underground and live on earthworms, grubs, and other invertebrates. (Some moles also nibble on parts of plants.) The mole's body is built for tunneling, tapered at both ends like a football. The mole's eyes are tiny and its ears don't stick out so dirt doesn't often get in either place. Most important, a mole's forelimbs have formidable claws for powerful digging.

mole

This common bird species did not arrive in North America until 1890. In that year, fifteen pairs of European starlings were set free in New York state. Over the next hundred years, those thirty birds, and their offspring, have increased the starling population in North America one millionfold. Starlings can now be found in every state of the U.S., and they have thrived at the expense of many native species of birds. Today, many people regard starlings as pests because they drive other birds away and because they eat berries and fruit.

no teeth · big gulp

swallowing whole and headfirs

· fur · Boreal Owl · glandula

stomach · mucus · enzyme

· acids · feathers · Saw-Whet Owl

muscular stomac

· grinding and straining · bones

absorbing nutrients · Spotted O

· nature's "trash compactor"

producing pellet

· Northern Hawk Owl · regurgitatio

· gag me · owl puke!

no taste · bug shelters · ne

package · other bird barf · flexib

esophagus · gizzard · ga

CHAPTER FOUR

OWL PUKE

NCE AN OWL HAS CAUGHT its prey, it positions the animal headfirst in its beak. Then, with a few upward thrusts with its head and neck, an owl swallows the meal whole, in one big gulp. The prey's skin, fur, or feathers protects the owl's throat as the food makes its way down the bird's long, flexible esophagus.

Owls swallow their small prey whole, but the birds can't digest fur, fins, feathers, and bones. Producing pellets is a special

OTHER BIRD BARF

The food that some birds store in their crops comes in handy when it's time to feed the kids. Many bird parents—including penguins, doves, and herons—regurgitate food directly into their babies' mouths to feed them. But seagulls vomit on their nests, and the little gulls help themselves!

way owls have to get rid of prey parts they can't digest.

Owls' efficient eating methods enable them to eat many rodents, birds, and other animals in a single evening. But how does an owl separate the meat of its prey from all the other parts an owl can't digest?

Nature has provided owls with an ingenious way of separating the meat of their prey from its bone, hair, fur, or feathers.

DOUBLE DUTY DIGESTION

A N OWL'S STOMACH has two parts. Sliding down an owl's throat, prey first lands in the proventriculus, or glandular stomach.

The proventriculus produces enzymes and acids, chemicals that dissolve and break up the body of the prey. The stomach also contains a lining of slippery mucus, just like the slimy stuff in your body, that helps prevent strong stomach acids from dissolving a hole in your gut. In an owl, mucus helps move the mess of flesh and bones up to the second part of the stomach, called the *gizzard*, or muscular stomach.

MARVELOUS MUCUS

They may not blow big, wet sneezes, but owls have mucus just like humans. In people, mucus is that slippery stuff that comes out of your nose and sticks in your throat when you have a cold (it's your body's very own germ catcher), lines your stomach, and lubricates lots of other organs so they can function.

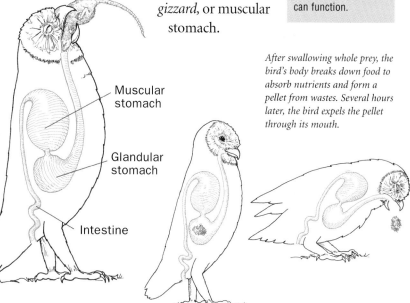

After swallowing whole prey, the bird's body breaks down food to absorb nutrients and form a pellet from wastes. Several hours later, the bird expels the pellet through its mouth.

Muscular stomach

Glandular stomach

Intestine

gak!

OWL INVESTIGATIONS

Quick Quiz

Barn Owls usually produce . . .

A. two pellets a day

B. five pellets a day

C. ten pellets a day

D. two pellets a week

(Answer is at the bottom of this page)

The gizzard works like a strainer to catch claws, bones, teeth, fur, and feathers—the animal parts the owl cannot digest. With powerful muscle contractions, the gizzard grinds up the meat of the prey. Those soluble, or soft food, parts pass through the small intestine, which absorbs nutrients and water, into the large intestine, then to an area called the cloaca. The cloaca holds wastes, fecal matter, that the bird releases by way of a vent.

While the owl is digesting its meal, all the indigestible material remains in the gizzard. There, the muscular stomach is hard at work, pressing hair, feathers, and fur around bones

(ANSWER: A)

to form a nice, neat package: a gizzard-shaped owl pellet. This work can take several hours.

OWL PUKE

ONCE THE PELLET IS FINISHED forming in the gizzard, it travels back to the proventriculus. The pellet may stay there for up to ten hours.

Regurgitation occurs when the owl's digestive system has finished absorbing all the food nutrients from its meal and the owl is ready to eat again. Owls puke on a regular cycle, usually leaving pellets in the same place each time.

When the owl is ready to get rid of the pellet, it closes its eyes. Then the bird stretches its neck up and forward, its stomach contracts, and out drops the pellet.

Scientists believe owls have little or no sense of taste. Owls probably don't taste the food when it's going down, or the pellet coming up.

Once the bird has regurgitated, the pellet remains in the owl's habitat—in a barn, on a forest floor, in a rock crevice, in the desert or tundra or anywhere the owl lives.

But the pellet doesn't just sit there. Owl pellets may be waste to an owl, but to other animals and fungi, they're real treasures.

NATURE'S OWN TRASH COMPACTOR

If you put a piece of sandwich bread in your hand, and continuously close and open your fingers around it, the bread gets squashed, right? Well, if you keep doing it, pretty soon you'll have a small, smooth nugget of gray doughy stuff in your palm. That's how an owl's gizzard works—as a kind of trash compactor. Its strong muscles contract, compressing parts of prey the owl can't process— usually from several different animals— into a smooth package of puke!

TO HURL OR NOT TO HURL

When a Barn Owl hawks up a pellet, it's a rather dainty drop, not wretched retching. On the other hand, other owl species really know how to hurl. Some species open and shut their beaks, shake their heads vigorously for five or more minutes...then let the pellet fly.

Pellets provide shelter and food for beetles, moths, and other organisms that move into their bone-filled new home—and may stay there for generations.

SAME OWL SPECIES, DIFFERENT OWL PELLET

EVER TRY FROG'S LEGS, camel's feet, or a whole sheep's head? No? What about fried dragonflies, skewered scorpions, or maggot cheese? Still no? Well, how about a fresh bloodshake or some rancid yak milk to wash down your meal? No again? Many people around the world happily eat these things— and might even think your bologna and cheese with mayo is the grossest thing around.

People eat what is available—different environments mean different diets. It works that way for owls of the same species, too. All Barn Owls eat mammals, birds, reptiles, and amphibians. But the creatures they eat vary widely by habitat.

For example, if you dissected a Barn Owl pellet from Africa, you might find skeletons of the great cane rat, a species that weighs fifteen pounds. Barn Owl pellets from other places in the world may contain the bones of bats, fish, and frogs.

FULLY LOADED PELLETS

Our pellets are superior!

OTHER RAPTORS PRODUCE pellets, but owl pellets contain more bones and other interesting evidence of what the birds have eaten. Why?

Unlike owls, who swallow prey whole, hawks, eagles, and other birds of prey tear at their food, leaving the bones—so their pellets don't contain skeletons. Additionally, owls' digestive juices are less acidic than those of other raptors. That means they break down hard food less efficiently, so their pellets contain more fur and other materials. Finally, because owls don't have crops to hold excess food, they regurgitate pellets more frequently.

All of this adds up to the fact that owl pellets are loaded with more interesting things than those of other birds.

INSIDE OWL PUKE

YOU'LL USUALLY FIND more than one skeleton in a single owl pellet because the bird eats many times in a single evening. Many bones collect in the owl's gizzard, and are formed into a single pellet.

NO CROP

Other birds have a loose sac in their throats called a *crop* where they store food to eat and digest at a later time. Owls don't have a crop, so what they catch and eat is what they digest— right away.

Almost Everybody Pukes

HUMANS

Vomiting is your body's way of getting rid of what ails you, from too many chili dogs to harmful bacteria. Your brain tells your esophagus, or throat, to open up, directs your muscular diaphragm to bear down on your stomach, and closes entry to your intestines and windpipe—so you don't inhale that slimy stuff.

From there the contents of your stomach—the good, bad, and ugly—go up and out.

CATS

Cats heave hairballs, slimy, sausage-shaped wads of soggy hair. When cats lick their fur, some of that fur falls out, sticks to their rough tongues, and ends up in their stomachs.

That hair collects and compresses to form a felty wad. When it gets too big, out it comes.

FROGS

Some frog species take a whole different approach to puking—literally spewing their guts. When these frogs eat something that disagrees with them, they hurl their whole stomachs. After wiping off the organ with a leg, the frogs just swallow their stomachs up again—and they're back in business.

To "puke" is to vomit. It means to disgorge the contents of a stomach through the mouth. A startled snake might vomit a mouse. Whales have been known to vomit squid. Now that you know owl pellets inside and out, have a look at how other animals puke:

SEA CUCUMBERS

Not a vegetable at all, but a slimy ocean animal, this "slug o' the sea" can get huge—over six feet long. To surprise and distract predators, sea cucumbers actually toss their tummies, puking their *whole stomachs* into the water. While the predator snacks on those soft bits of sea cucumber stomach, the creature slips away. How does that seafaring, sluglike animal survive? Over several months, it regrows its internal organs.

VULTURES

If you eat dead, decaying things, your breath isn't exactly a bouquet of roses. And if you're a vulture, your vomit becomes your secret weapon.

To distract predators vultures spew chunks of rotting meat, stewed in gastric juices. A little of that puke can go a long way—some turkey vultures can hit a target with projectile vomit from six feet away.

Vomiting gives vultures a bonus: it makes them lighter so they can make a fast escape.

NO PUKE PROBLEM

Although puking may not always be the most pleasant way to spend your spare time, it serves many important purposes for both humans and other animals. Horses, rodents, and rabbits can't vomit— which means they have big problems if they eat something poisonous that other animals could get rid of by puking.

mysterious clues • straw
owl pellet journal • insect home
• observation • go slow!
pick away • skulls • toothpick
• tooth clues • sorting
look closely! • tiny piece
• fur fluff • bone-sorting tray
vertebrae • ribs • jaw
• water • identifying bones
hips • legs • reconstructi
skeletons • wash your hands
magnifying glass • investigat
• tweezers • newspaper • incisor
• sign your creatio

CHAPTER FIVE

DISCOVER SKELETONS

DISSECTING AN OWL PELLET is a bit like solving a mystery. You search for clues, sift through evidence, and finally put the pieces of your investigation together. Your mission? To use your knowledge of owls and observation, dissection, and identification skills to determine a Barn Owl's prey, based on bones you find. Like any good detective, you'll need to do advance work before beginning your investigation to uncover the skeleton—or skeletons—within.

STEP ONE:
Setting Up

WHAT YOU'LL NEED

- one sterilized owl pellet
- toothpicks to use as dissecting tools
- newspaper to cover and protect your tabletop
- plastic bone-sorting tray (or compartmented paper plate)

OPTIONAL

- cup of water
- tweezers
- magnifying glass
- notebook or paper and pen for recording observations
- sealable plastic bags

FOR LATER

To assemble one of your pellet's skeletons, you'll need:

- colored construction paper (8½" x 11")
- white glue

To start, find a place to work where your investigation won't be disturbed. Some cats and dogs are extremely interested in owl pellets—from sniffing at them to tearing them apart—so make sure your workspace is out of your pet's reach.

Lay down a sheet of newspaper on your workspace and assemble your pellet and tools. If you wish, put a plain piece of white paper to the side of the newspaper. As you separate bones from other materials, you can place them on this paper. Bones show up better against white paper than they do on newspaper and are less likely to get lost if you can see them.

Remove bone labels and place them on the compartments of the plastic bone-sorting tray. Each compartment should have a separate label.

If you wish, grab a notebook and a pen to record your observations. You're now ready to begin your owl pellet investigation.

Don't dissect owl pellets you find in the wild!

STEP TWO:

Observation

Carefully unwrap the foil-covered pellet. What do you see on its surface? Feathers, fur, or both? Dirt, straw, hay, seeds, grass, or pine needles? These things are clues that can tell you about where the owl lives and what it eats.

Unsterilized owl pellets may contain nasty germs that can make you sick.

JOURNAL

OWL PELLET

ENTRY No. 1

Create a lasting record of your owl pellet investigation with an Owl Pellet Journal.

First entry: Make a life-size sketch of your pellet, noting interesting features.

Excavation

You can use a little water to soften your pellet.

Now that you've carefully examined the owl pellet, you're ready to begin dissecting it. The key to successful pellet excavation is working slowly and carefully, so you don't break or overlook bones.

Using a toothpick, gently begin taking apart the pellet. Start at a place on the pellet where bones may be visible on the outside, and carefully pull back the dark covering a little at a time to reveal the bone. If you can't see any bones from the outside, start by picking or tweezing a small area of the pellet until you begin to see something inside.

You can also use the toothpick to drill down into the pellet until you hit something hard. Pick away at the hole you've made until you uncover a bone.

Carefully break your pellet apart.

As you find bones, put them into a separate pile.

If the pellet is very hard and difficult to pull apart, dampen it with water to soften it. You can also soak excavated bones in a cup of water to remove fur and other materials that may cling.

Continue to separate bones from other matter. Move bones to one side of your workspace.

Pellet dissection is slow, careful work and can take a long time—so you don't have to do it all at once. If you want to stop excavating and come back to it later, put bones in one sealable plastic bag and the rest of the pellet and other materials in another, and return to your investigation when you have time.

JOURNAL

OWL PELLET

ENTRY No.2

You may find more than one skull in a pellet. The number of skulls tells you how many prey your owl ate before it puked. Note the number in your journal. Did the owl eat different kinds of prey? Or are the skulls two of a kind?

STEP FOUR:

Skull
Examination

WHAT IS IT?

IF THE SKULL HAS . . .

NO TEETH, go to **1**.

NO INCISORS: if teeth are in ridges like an alligator, go to **2**; if front teeth are forward pointing and cheek teeth are reddish, go to **3**.

INCISORS: if cheek teeth are in a zigzag pattern, go to **4**; if the jaw is more than half an inch long, go to **5**; if the jaw is less than half an inch long, go to **6**.

1. It's a bird.
2. It's a mole.
3. It's a shrew.
4. It's a vole.
5. It's a rat.
6. It's a mouse.

Look CAREFULLY at the skull. The shape of the skull, and especially its teeth, can help you identify the prey in the pellet. Compare the skull to the Bone Sorting Chart or the key at left to determine what, exactly, you've found.

CHEEK TEETH   **INCISOR**

JOURNAL

OWL PELLET

ENTRY **No.3**

Create an Owl Pellet Detection data sheet to record your finds. This might include total numbers of:

____ prey found
____ birds found
____ rodents found
____ shrews found
____ moles found
____ insects found

STEP FIVE:

Bone Identification

Once you've identified the animal, use the Bone Sorting Chart to identify the other bones. See if you can find the creature's jaw. (If your pellet has more than one skull, which jaw matches which skull? Check the Bone Sorting Chart to be sure.) Next, you can look for other large bones that once made up the animal's legs. Finally, see if you can find ribs and vertebrae, the tiny bones that make up creatures' necks, backs, and tails.

Keep checking your bones as you sort. (Using a magnifying glass can help you see the smallest bones better.) To store your sorted bones, place them in the labeled compartments of your bone-sorting tray. Slip the tray into a plastic bag and seal until you are ready to reconstruct your skeletons. Remember to wash your hands if you are done for the day.

Always wash your hands after working with owl pellets!

BONE SORT

Use this chart to organize and identify the bones you fin

	SKULL	JAWS	SHOULDER BLADES	FRONT LEGS
RODENT				
SHREW				
MOLE				
BIRD				WINGS
OTHER	Caterpillar larvae and cocoons			

your pellet!

HIPS	BACK LEGS	RIBS	VERTEBRAE

Caterpillar droppings

STEP SIX:

Skeleton Reconstruction

OWL PELLET

ENTRY No. 4

Write about the owl that produced your pellet and the prey you found inside. Give the bird a name and describe its family and home. Then, write about the day it went hunting, including how it captured and ate its prey and produced the pellet you've dissected.

Using the Skeleton Reconstruction Chart on page 71 as a guide, you can create a full skeleton from the bones you've found. Here's how:

One: Once you've collected all skeletal parts and have stored them in the bone-sorting tray, clear your workspace of stray fur, feathers, and other materials. To make your skeleton, you'll need bones from your pellet, a piece of construction or other sturdy colored paper, and white glue.

Two: Using a pencil, pen, or crayon, copy the Skeleton Reconstruction Chart on the paper. This will become your guide for placing bones on the paper.

Three: Choose and identify a skull from your sorted bones.

Four: Referring back to the Skeleton Reconstruction Chart and using your outline as a guide, choose bones and assemble them on the construction paper in the appropriate places. Be careful—as you can see, some of the bones are tiny and easy to lose.

Five: Once you have the right bones in the right places, use white glue to attach them to the paper. Put in a safe place to dry for several hours.

Six: You now have your very own recon-structed skeleton, suitable for displaying proudly. If you like, you can label the bones on your work with a pen, just as a scientist would. And of course, sign your creation.

Oh, the leg bone's connected to the hip bone ...

MAJOR BONES

You'll find these bones in an owl pellet:

- Skull, including the upper jaw or maxilla
- Jaw (mandible)
- Shoulder blades (scapulae)
- Forelimbs, or front legs, consisting of the humerus, radius, and ulna
- Hips (pelvis)
- Hindlimbs, or back legs, consisting of the femur, fibula, and tibia
- Ribs

. . . along with five kinds of vertebrae:

- Cervical vertebrae (neck)
- Thoracic vertebrae (chest)
- Lumbar vertebrae (abdominal)
- Sacral vertebrae (attaches the backbone to the pelvis)
- Caudal vertebrae (tail)

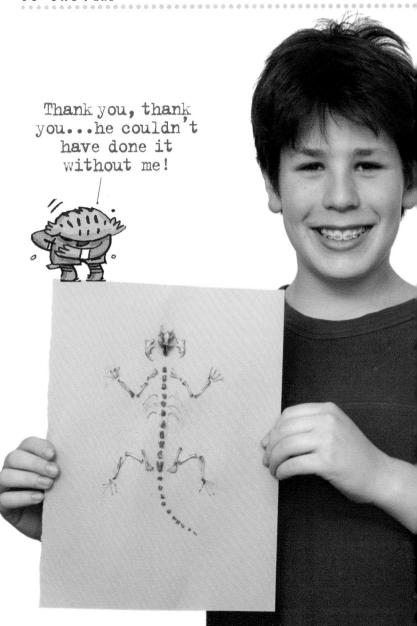

Rodent
SKELETON RECONSTRUCTION CHART

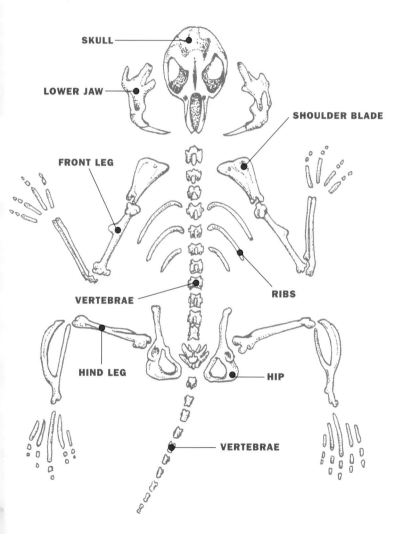

SKULL

LOWER JAW

SHOULDER BLADE

FRONT LEG

VERTEBRAE

RIBS

HIND LEG

HIP

VERTEBRAE

edible owl pellets

where to see owls • make awesome ea

tufts • puking owl card • wildli

rehabilitation • Queen Solomo

• owl profiles • "adopt" an owl

raptor centers • zo

• find out more • acknowledgments

glossary • dissect another pell

• cow's cud • shark puke

worm gizzard • why people don't ma

pellets • rat bones • bird bon

• what's a skeleton?

neckless moles • your bone

• barn owls live in barns • it's a hoo

CHAPTER SIX

OWL ACTIVITIES

(AND OTHER COOL STUFF)

ATTENTION, PELLET PICKERS! Now that you're kn*owl*-edgeable about amazing birds of prey and have successfully conducted a real science investigation, it's time for more fun—owl-style fun, that is. From ideas on where to find owls and tips on how to talk with them to complete instructions for making your own edible owl pellets and a cool puking owl card; from jokes about our favorite birds to incredible owl myths—you'll find lots more to explore here. So turn the page and "dig in." It's a hoot!

EDIBLE OWL PELLETS

THESE LOOK AMAZINGLY LIKE THE REAL THING but taste great! Chock-full of crunchy "bone" bits, these no-bake, chocolaty nuggets are easy to make.

INGREDIENTS:

6 cups crispy rice cereal

2 cups (12 ounces) semisweet or milk chocolate chips

1 cup sugar

1 cup corn syrup

1 cup peanut butter (either smooth or crunchy, which adds "authentic" texture!)

1 white chocolate or "cookies and cream" candy bar, chopped into bonelike bits (about ⅓ cup)

foil for wrapping pellets

Chocolate Barn Owl Pellets

(makes about 36 servings)

1. In a large bowl, mix cereal and chocolate chips. Set aside.

2. Mix sugar and corn syrup in a small pan, and heat until hot and bubbling. (Have an adult assist you.)

3. Remove sugar-syrup mixture from heat and stir in peanut butter.

4. Stir peanut butter mixture into cereal and chocolate chips, and mix together well. (The chocolate chips will melt.) When cereal is completely coated, allow mixture to sit for five minutes to cool.

5. Using washed hands, pick up 2–3 tablespoons of the mixture. Sprinkle 4–5 white chocolate "bones" into the mixture in your hand.

6. Squeeze mixture in your fist until it looks just like an owl pellet. Smooth edges if necessary, and place chocolate "pellet" on a plate.

7. Wrap each pellet in foil and store in refrigerator. Enjoy digging in!

BE AN OWL . . . OR JUST LOOK LIKE ONE

FORGET MOUSE EARS. (Who really wants to look like a rodent, anyway?) Instead, try dressing in real raptor style, with a set of owlish ear tufts. You can be the hit of the Halloween party, or scare your friends anytime by wearing these in public . . . because nothing says "owl crazy" like a fine pair of feathery faux ears.

1. Select the feathers you want to use for your ear tufts.

2. Position feathery ear tufts on the hair band and attach with glue. Allow to dry.

3. Well done. Place your new ear tufts on your head and get out there and hoot at someone!

WHAT YOU'LL NEED:

- colored feathers from a craft store (look for real-life owl colors, like white, gray, brown, and beige, unless you're feeling really wacky—then anything goes!)
- a plastic hairband—any type will work fine
- glue or rubber cement

Step 2   *Step 3*

PUKING OWL CARD

WHEN YOU OPEN THE CARD, the owl inside opens its beak wide!

WHAT YOU'LL NEED:

- two pieces of construction paper, card stock, or other sturdy paper
- glue
- scissors
- markers, pens, or crayons

1. Fold both pieces of paper in half. Set aside one piece of paper. That will be the outside of the card.

2. Take the other folded piece of paper. One-third of the way down the fold, cut a straight, 1½-inch line.

3. Fold back each side to form two triangles.

4. Open the card. Place it on your work surface faceup, like an open book.

5. Push one of the triangles forward and pinch the crease, so it sticks up above the card. Repeat with the other triangle so the two triangles form a beak.

6. Close the card and press the folds, so creases are sharp. Open the card—that's your owl's beak popping open!

Step 5

Step 7

Step 8

7. Lay the uncut piece of paper faceup, like an open book on your work surface. Glue the cut piece of paper inside it, lining up edges. Let dry.

8. Draw an owl around the beak. (You can even include a little pellet on the ground next to the bird!)

9. Presto! You've just finished a one-of-a-kind "gag" card. Open and close the card to watch its beak open wide!

Queen Solomon is a Great Horned Owl at Wind Over Wings, a wildlife rehabilitation and education center in Clinton, Connecticut. A woman found her as an owlet and raised her on bread. When the bird got too big to keep, the woman brought her to Wind Over Wings. Trained experts could care for the owl for rerelease into the wild.

Sadly, the owl's poor diet and the fact that she had been imprinted on humans meant the bird would not be able to survive anywhere else. Today, Queen Solomon visits schools with Wind Over Wings, but she will never be able to fly freely through the woods as other Great Horned Owls do.

WHERE TO SEE OWLS

THERE ARE LOTS of ways to find out where owls live in your area. Ask your teacher or librarian for help. Look in your local newspaper for notices of nature walks and bird watching. Check your regional Audubon Society for wildlife sanctuaries and your nearest zoo for birds of prey. The science departments at state universities are often terrific sources of local information. So are retail stores that specialize in birdseed and feeders.

You may have a raptor center near you. Raptor centers are places where all kinds of birds of prey are studied. Some centers rehabilitate birds (visit the Raptor Education Group, Inc. at www.raptoreducationgroup. org to learn more), and some centers have special hours for visitors.

Contact a raptor center near you for more information:

The Raptor Center at Auburn University
Auburn, Alabama
www.vetmed.auburn.edu/raptor

Alaska Raptor Center
Sitka, Alaska
www.alaskaraptor.org

California Raptor Center
School of Veterinary Medicine
University of California
Davis, California
www.vetmed.ucdavis.edu/ars/raptor

Wildcare
The Terwilliger Center for Nature Education and Wildlife Rehabilitation
San Rafael, California
www.wildcaremarin.org

Predatory Bird Research Group
Long Marine Lab
University of California
Santa Cruz, California
www2.ucsc.edu/scpbrg

Birds of Prey Foundation
Broomfield, Colorado
www.birds-of-prey.org

Earthplace
Westport, Connecticut
www.earthplace.org

Audubon Center for Birds of Prey
Maitland, Florida
www.audubonofflorida.org/conservation

World Center for Birds of Prey
Boise, Idaho
www.peregrinefund.org

The Illinois Raptor Center
Decatur, Illinois
www.illinoisraptorcenter.org

S.O.A.R. (Save Our American Raptors)
Earlville, Illinois
www.soar-inc.org

Macbride Raptor Project
Kirkwood Community College
Cedar Rapids, Iowa
and the University of Iowa's Macbride Nature Recreation Area
www.macbrideraptorproject.org

The Raptor Center
University of Minnesota
St. Paul, Minnesota
www.raptor.cvm.umn.edu

World Bird Sanctuary
Valley Park, Missouri
www.worldbirdsanctuary.org

The Raptor Trust
Millington, New Jersey
www.theraptortrust.org

Raptor Center
Frost Valley YMCA
Claryville, New York
www.frostvalley.org

"ADOPT" AN OWL

Although owls make terrible pets to keep at home, many nature sanctuaries and wildlife rehabilitation centers have programs that allow you to "adopt" one of these incredible birds of prey. Your support often covers the costs of the bird's food and medical care, so that injured birds can heal and eventually return to the wild. To find out more, talk to someone at your local wildlife center about "adopting" an owl.

Braddock Bay Raptor Research
Hilton, New York
www.bbrr.com

Hudson Valley Raptor Center
Stanfordville, New York

Carolina Raptor Center
Huntersville, North Carolina
www.birdsofprey.org

Raptor Center Glen Helen Ecology Institute
Yellow Springs, Ohio
www.glenhelen.org

Cascades Raptor Center
Eugene, Oregon
www.raptor-center.com

Hawk Mountain Sanctuary Association
Kempton, Pennsylvania
www.hawkmountain.org

Raptor Center Shaver's Creek Environmental Center
Penn State
Petersburg, Pennsylvania
www.shaverscreek.org

Raptor Center Heard Natural Science Museum and Wildlife Sanctuary
McKinney, Texas
www.heardmuseum.org/heardraptor

Raptor Center Vermont Institute of Natural Science
Quechee, Vermont
www.vinsweb.org

The Raptor Conservancy of Virginia
Falls Church, Virginia
www.raptorsva.org

O.W.L. (Orphaned Wildlife Rehabilitation Society)
Delta, British Columbia
Canada
www.owlcanada.ca

Many zoos have excellent birds of prey exhibits. Here are some where you can see owls:

Denver Zoo
Denver, Colorado
www.denverzoo.org

Lincoln Park Zoo
Chicago, Illinois
www.lpzoo.org

Louisville Zoological Garden
Louisville, Kentucky
www.louisvillezoo.org

Como Park Zoo
St. Paul, Minnesota
www.ci.stpaul.mn.us/
depts/parks/comopark

Bronx Zoo
Bronx, New York
www.bronxzoo.org

Cincinnati Zoo
Cincinnati, Ohio
www.cincyzoo.org

Oregon Zoo
Portland, Oregon
www.zooregon.org

Fort Worth Zoo
Fort Worth, Texas
www.fortworthzoo.org

Woodland Park Zoo
Seattle, Washington
www.zoo.org

WHERE TO BUY OWL PELLETS

ONE OF AMERICA'S PREMIERE PELLET SUPPLIERS is Pellets, Inc. of Bellingham, Washington. You can reach Pellets, Inc. toll-free at 1-888-466-OWLS. You can also order pellets on-line at www.pelletsinc.com. The minimum order is ten pellets.

MINI PROFILES

OWLS OF NORTH AMERICA

The Barn Owl is distinguished by its heart-shaped face and long legs. These birds roost and nest in barns, silos, and old houses.

The Flammulated Owl is a migratory species, spending the winter in Mexico. For habitat, they prefer pine, fir, and aspen forests.

The Eastern Screech Owl roosts and nests in wooded habitats. Its feeding ranges include suburban lawns and urban-area open spaces.

The Western Screech Owl is equally at home in the tropical lowlands of the Baja Peninsula and the temperate rain forests of British Columbia and southern Alaska.

The Spotted Owl inhabits some of the oldest remaining forests in North America.

The Great Horned Owl lives in nearly every kind of habitat in North America. Hunting areas are open fields or marshes with trees for perching.

The Snowy Owl lives for most of the year in one of the harshest habitats on Earth: the far north.

The Elf Owl is the smallest owl in North America, standing only six inches tall. Its high-pitched call sounds like a puppy yelping.

The Burrowing Owl likes open fields with low grass. Although Burrowing Owls have been known to dig holes, most nest in prairie dog towns or in other holes dug by rodents.

The Barred Owl lives in heavy woods near open fields. Like other forest owls, the Barred prefers old growth woods.

The Great Gray Owl is the largest owl in North America (standing more than two feet tall).

The Long-Eared Owl likes open spaces for hunting with nearby woods for roosting.

The Northern Saw-Whet Owl typically roosts among dense, young evergreens at the edge of large woods. The owl hunts in both woods and open fields.

The Short-Eared Owl is a courtship daredevil. To attract a mate, the male takes off into the air, rapidly climbing with rhythmic strokes and clapping its wings.

The Boreal Owl mainly lives in pine forests where it may be found standing motionless on a low branch. The Boreal mostly hunts with its ears and plunges into shrubs to capture hidden prey.

Stomachs and Digestion

Owls have an unusual digestive system. Do you know how other systems work?

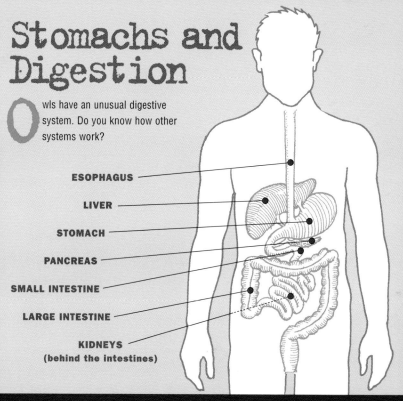

ESOPHAGUS

LIVER

STOMACH

PANCREAS

SMALL INTESTINE

LARGE INTESTINE

KIDNEYS
(behind the intestines)

HUMANS

As you eat, your teeth break down the food, mixing it with saliva (also known as spit). When you swallow, a flap called the epiglottis closes off access to your windpipe, and the chewed food passes down the esophagus into your stomach. There, the food gets churned up with digestive juices and acids, forming food mush. This mush then passes to the duodenum, the entrance to the small intestine. The mush gets mixed up with more digestive liquid, this time from the liver and pancreas.

As the mush passes through the small intestine, nutrients are absorbed into the bloodstream. Next, it's into the large intestine, where water from the mush is absorbed. Liquid waste is filtered by the kidneys and turned into urine. Solid waste ends up in the rectum, which leads to the anus, the muscled exit to the outside world.

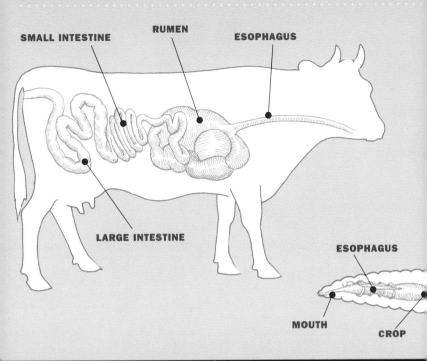

SMALL INTESTINE

RUMEN

ESOPHAGUS

LARGE INTESTINE

ESOPHAGUS

MOUTH

CROP

RUMINANTS

Cows, goats, sheep, buffalo, deer, antelope, elks, yaks, and camels all have hooves, eat plants, and are ruminants. Ruminants have not just one, but four stomach chambers that enable the animals to digest grasses and other plants.

After a goat or other ruminant takes a big chomp of grass, it travels to the first stomach section, the rumen. There, food mixes with bacteria, forming a gooey mass called a bolus, or cud. The animal regurgitates the cud back into its mouth and the cud is slowly chewed, for hours, and eventually swallowed.

WORMS

Worms don't have stomachs, but they digest food, too. Once an earthworm has sucked in a snack of dirt or decaying plants with its mouth and pharynx, or muscular throat, it travels down the esophagus. Some food is stored in the animal's crop to process later; the rest moves on to the gizzard, which grinds up the food.

Next the food moves along to the tube-shaped intestine, the alimentary canal, that runs the whole length of the worm. There, chemicals further break down the food, and nutrients are absorbed. Waste materials pass out of the worm's body through the anus.

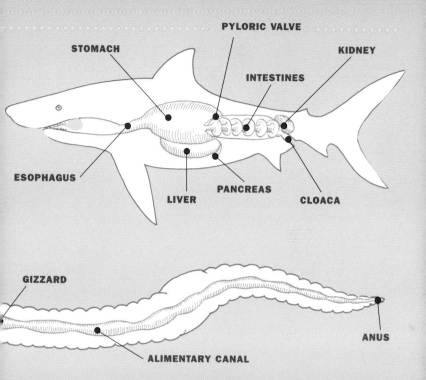

STOMACH

PYLORIC VALVE

KIDNEY

INTESTINES

ESOPHAGUS

LIVER

PANCREAS

CLOACA

GIZZARD

ANUS

ALIMENTARY CANAL

SHARKS

With huge jaws and several rows of supersharp teeth, meat-eating sharks tear at large aquatic prey, swallowing large chunks of flesh and bones. Food travels down the animal's wide esophagus to its stomach, which expands to hold big prey.

To break down large meals, a shark produces powerful stomach enzymes in its pancreas. A shark's pancreas is much larger than those of other vertebrates. Acids and enzymes in the animal's stomach break down food into a soupy consistency.

The soupy liquid moves through the pyloric valve, which separates the shark's stomach from its intestines. Any large bones and other materials that the shark can't digest are vomited out into the ocean.

The shark's folded intestines have a large surface area that efficiently absorbs nutrients. Waste leaves the body through an opening called the cloaca, just as it does with owls.

Bones and Skeletons

How are you like a rat—deep in your bones? How is your skeletal structure different from that of other animals? How might you look if you could fly, tunnel underground, or run on four legs? Compare and contrast the skeletons here to find out how your bones stack up against others.

BIRD BONES

Most birds have lightweight, hollow bones that are perfectly suited for flight. (The exception is flightless birds, such as penguins, who are remarkably equipped with flipperlike wings for propelling themselves through water, rather than through the air.) Although they have flexible necks, birds have fixed backbones, which provide stability when they fly.

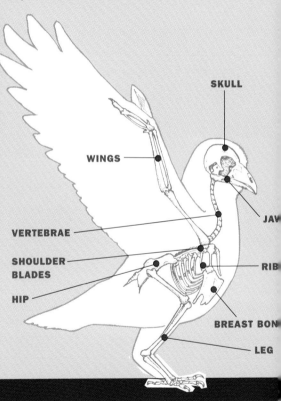

SKULL

WINGS

JAW

VERTEBRAE

SHOULDER BLADES

HIP

RIB

BREAST BONE

LEG

OWLS

With hollow bones for easy flight, an owl's lightweight forelimbs form its wings. Long hindlimb bones give an owl strength for catching prey. Wide eye sockets (known as orbits) accommodate the animal's large eyes—which, if they were in a human, would be the size of grapefruits!

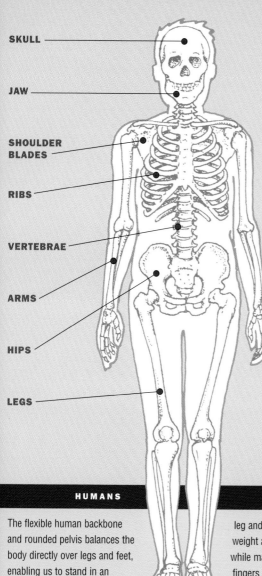

SKULL

JAW

SHOULDER
BLADES

RIBS

VERTEBRAE

ARMS

HIPS

LEGS

WHAT'S A SKELETON?

Coral is a skeleton. So are crab claws and oyster shells. Even plants have skeletons.

Some skeletons are *exoskeletons*, growing on the outside of an animal. Others are internal skeletons, or *endoskeletons,* which are found inside an organism. A skeleton is the frame that supports, maintains, and protects the organs of living things.

HUMANS

The flexible human backbone and rounded pelvis balances the body directly over legs and feet, enabling us to stand in an upright position. Long, strong leg and foot bones support body weight and propel forward movement while maintaining balance. Arms and fingers are adapted for precise movement and grip.

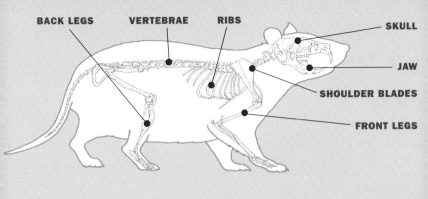

BACK LEGS   VERTEBRAE   RIBS   SKULL   JAW   SHOULDER BLADES   FRONT LEGS

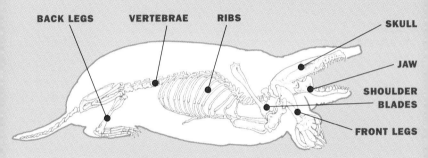

BACK LEGS   VERTEBRAE   RIBS   SKULL   JAW   SHOULDER BLADES   FRONT LEGS

Note: In most mammals, the collarbone is connected to the shoulder blade. But in moles, the collarbone connects directly to its upper arm. This makes moles look neckless.

RATS (TOP)	MOLES (BOTTOM)
Like most rodents, rats have five digits on their forelimbs to hold food; powerful, large hind limbs for jumping; and long tails to maintain balance. Able to move fast using all four feet, rats and other rodents can sometimes escape predators such as owls. With powerful jaw bones and muscles that enable them to chew through materials as solid as concrete, rats are well adapted to a life of foraging.	These animals don't need back legs for standing and jumping or tails for balancing. The most prominent feature of a mole skeleton is the large shovel-shaped claw on each forelimb. The forelimbs themselves are short and strong and have an unusual structure. The elbows point upward and the palms of the front claws face toward the back. A mole's skeletal structure results in a breaststroke motion as the mole digs.

GLOSSARY

Adaptation: adjustments to conditions or surroundings that a species makes over time

Binocular: a type of vision in which both eyes see the same image, enabling an animal to judge distance and speed

Brood patch: the featherless area on a bird's body where eggs are kept warm before hatching

Carnivore: a meat eater

Cloaca: the area in owls and other animals where wastes are stored before elimination

Clutch: the group of eggs a bird lays

Cone cell: a light-sensitive cell in the eye that distinguishes color

Courtship: a behavior pattern that leads to mating

Crop: an organ that stores food until the stomach is ready to accommodate it (most birds have a crop, but owls do not)

Diurnal: active during the day

Ear tufts: not ears, but the feathers on some owl species that resemble ears

Egg tooth: a small, sharp beak tip that baby owls and other birds use during hatching to chip out of shells

Esophagus: the muscular tube that connects the mouth to the stomach

Facial disk: a disk of facial feathers that owls move to direct sound into the ears

Fledge: to grow the feathers necessary for flight

Food chain/web: the interrelationships among animals and plants involving the transfer of food energy

Gizzard: the muscular part of owls' and other animals' stomachs where food is ground up and strained in the digestion process, and where owl pellets are formed

Habitat: the environment where an animal lives

Herbivore: a plant eater

Home territory: the area a bird inhabits

Incubate: to keep eggs warm by sitting on them until they hatch

GLOSSARY (CONTINUED)

Imprinting: the process of a young animal developing a bond and identifying with another of the same species

Mobbing: when crows and other birds threaten owls with calls, pecking, circling, and swooping

Molting: the process of losing and replacing feathers with new ones

Nictitating membrane: the third eyelid, or membrane, on birds and other animals that protects eyes while still allowing some vision

Nocturnal: active during the night

Omnivore: an animal that eats both plants and animals

Owlet: a young owl

Predator: an animal that feeds on other animals

Preen: to clean, straighten, or fluff feathers

Preen gland: see uropygial gland

Prey: an animal hunted by another animal for food

Proventriculus: the glandular stomach in owls and other animals where prey is first broken down in digestion and which stores owl pellets before regurgitation

Raptors: the group of birds of prey that includes owls, eagles, hawks, vultures, and other birds

Regurgitate: to bring food back up from the digestive tract after swallowing it, and expel it through the mouth

Rod cell: a light-sensitive cell important for seeing in dim light

Roost: a place where a bird sleeps, sometimes in groups

Species: a group of animals with shared characteristics that can reproduce and produce fertile offspring

Talons: claws

Uropygial gland: the oil-producing gland at the base of owls' and other birds' tails (also called a preen gland)

ACKNOWLEDGMENTS

SOME PARENT VOLUNTEERS get to bake brownies or help make pretty art projects. I got to help a group of grade-schoolers pick apart owl upchuck.

It was quite a sight. The kids in my son's classroom, from the worst behavior problems to the star students, from the prissiest of the prissy to the toughest of the tough guys, all suddenly became serious scientists. As they picked through the owl pellets and pulled out bones, as they expertly identified skulls and assembled skeletons, a cherub-faced child said something that summed it all up: "Owl puke is awesome."

Owl puke is awesome. So are owls. When my son and his friends wanted to dissect more owl pellets at home—like snowflakes, no two are ever alike—I gladly dug in with them. Those pellets led to more, and to a lot of questions about those amazing birds, what they eat, and why they produce such strange and fascinating pellets.

Which led to writing this book, and to meeting a lot of helpful people and birds. I'm especially grateful to Hope Douglas and Wind Over Wings, Walter Crawford of the World Bird Sanctuary, the crew at Earthplace, and teachers Pam Syndercombe and Jessica

Snajder, who cheerfully let me pick their brains about owl emesis. For help and humor along the way, I'd want Kathy Bishop, Donna Haupt, Alison Hendrie, Betsy Howie, and Debra Koenig in my flock any day. Huge hoot-outs go to Suzie Bolotin, whose enthusiasm and interest in retching raptors matched my own from the start, and to eagle-eyed agent Merrilee Heifetz of Writers House.

And of course, I'd never have gotten into the peculiarities of owl pellets in the first place if it weren't for Zachariah, Phineas, and Ezra Palmer, my family and partners in slime, grime, and scientific discoveries. Many thanks, guys.

I'll be seeing you,
hoo...hooo...hoooo...hooooooo